Vegan Christmas

The 100 tastiest recipes

for the

WINTER AND

CHRISTMAS TIME!

Valerja Rocha

Foreword

Welcome to this vegan cookbook. In this book, you will find a selection of the 100 best Christmas recipes. Whether simple butter biscuits or a more elaborate baked apple strudel. Of course, you can extend or modify the recipes. Just the way you like it!

I wish you good luck of course

Enjoy your meal!

Content

In advance - information about the recipes

- I have deliberately omitted recipe photos. They would increase the printing price of the book enormously and I could not offer this book for this price.

- The baking times given are based on my experience. Please note that deviations may occur more often.

- If you knead the dough with your hands, use cold vegan butter.

- Use vegan butter at room temperature with a food processor.

- Instead of vegan butter, vegan vegetable margarine can of course also be used.

- Of course, a fresh spice can also be used instead of powder.

Abbreviations

- TK = Frozen
- TL = teaspoon
- EL= tablespoon
- ml = millilitre

Soups

RED LENTIL COCONUT SOUP

Ingredients

400 ml coconut milk

700 ml vegetable stock

180 g red lentils, washed and drained

1 onion, diced

1 clove of garlic, pressed

1 carrot, sliced

2 tsp curry powder

2 tablespoons lemon juice

2 pinches pepper

some (rapeseed) oil for frying

Preparation

Heat the oil in a pot and sauté the onion, garlic, and curry powder for about 1 minute.

Add the lentils and carrot and steam briefly.

Deglaze with the vegetable stock and add coconut milk. Then bring to a boil.

Simmer gently for 25 minutes until the lentils break down and the vegetables are soft.

Now puree the soup and finely strain through a sieve.

Finally, season the soup with lemon juice and pepper.

PUMPKIN SOUP

Ingredients

500 g Hokkaido pumpkin, seeded and diced

700 ml vegetable soup

1 onion, finely chopped

1 clove of garlic, pressed

½ tsp ginger powder

1 pinch nutmeg

2 pinches pepper

1 pinch of salt

3 tbsp (rapeseed) oil

Pumpkin seed oil for drizzling

Preparation

Heat the oil in a pot and sauté the onion and garlic.
Add the pumpkin and steam briefly.
Deglaze with the vegetable stock and add the spices.
Bring to the boil and simmer gently for 25 minutes until the pumpkin is soft.
If the pumpkin soup is too thick, add some vegetable stock and bring it to the boil again briefly.
Puree the soup and serve drizzled with pumpkin seed oil.

VEGETABLE CREAM SOUP

Ingredients

5 Potato

400 g vegetables to taste (carrots, kohlrabi, peppers, etc.)

1 onion

1 clove of garlic

700 ml vegetable stock

½ tsp ginger powder

½ tsp pepper

½ tsp salt

2 tbsp (rapeseed) oil

1 tbsp parsley to garnish

Preparation

Cut the vegetables and potatoes into small cubes.

Press the garlic clove and dice the onion.

Heat the oil in a pot and sauté the onion and garlic until translucent.

Add the potatoes and vegetables and fry briefly.

Pour in the vegetable stock, bring to a boil and simmer for 30 minutes.

Puree the soup with a hand blender.

Serve the soup on a plate and garnish it with parsley.

TOMATOES - VEGETABLES SOUP

Ingredients

1 can of chopped tomatoes

1 can of strained tomatoes

3 carrots

1 onion

2 garlic cloves

1 leek

1 spring onion

1 courgette

1 tablespoon sugar

2 tbsp (coconut) oil

Salt to taste

Preparation

Cut the vegetables into small pieces, and press the garlic cloves.
Heat a pot with oil and fry the onion until translucent.

Add all ingredients except chopped tomatoes and simmer for 5 minutes.

Add the tomatoes to the pot and simmer on low heat for 20 minutes.

Puree the soup and season with salt.

BROCCOLI CREAM SOUP

Ingredients

1 broccoli

4 potatoes

1 onion

1 clove of garlic

800 ml vegetable stock

200 ml coconut milk

2 tbsp (rapeseed) oil

Salt to taste

Preparation

Dice the potatoes, chop the onion and press the garlic clove.
Heat a pot with oil and fry the onion until translucent.

Add the vegetable stock, garlic, and potatoes and cook in the closed pot for 10 minutes.

Meanwhile, cut off the broccoli florets and chop the stems.

Add the broccoli and coconut milk and cook for another 15 minutes.

Season with salt and bring to a boil again briefly.

CAULIFLOWER SOUP

Ingredients

1 cauliflower, in small pieces

1 potato, in small cubes

3 carrots, thinly sliced

2 onions, finely chopped

1 clove of garlic, pressed

700 ml vegetable stock

1 tsp curry powder

½ tsp ginger powder

2 pinches pepper

3 tbsp (rapeseed) oil

1 tbsp parsley to garnish

Preparation

Heat the oil in a pot and sauté the onion and garlic until translucent. Add the cauliflower and carrots and sauté briefly.

Deglaze with the vegetable stock, add the spices and simmer for 20 minutes.

Puree the soup with a hand blender.

If the soup is too thick, add a little water and bring it to a boil.

Serve the soup on a plate and garnish it with parsley.

BUCKWHEAT - PAPRIKA SOUP

Ingredients

100 g buckwheat

300 g potatoes

1 (red) pepper

1 Carrot

1 onion

1000 ml warm vegetable stock

250 ml soy cream

2 tbsp (rapeseed) oil

Salt to taste.

Preparation

Peel and wash the potatoes and cut them into small pieces.
Finely chop the onion and cut the pepper and carrot into small pieces.

Heat the oil in a high pan and fry the onion, pepper, and carrot for 3 minutes.

Add the vegetable stock, buckwheat, and potato and simmer for 30 minutes over medium heat.

Add the soy cream and simmer for another 10 minutes.

Season with salt and serve on deep plates.

BARLEY SOUP

Ingredients

150 g pearl barley (medium)

125 g smoked tofu, diced

5 potatoes, diced

1 small piece of celery, diced

2 carrots

1 onion, finely chopped

½ stick leek, cut into rings

1500 ml vegetable stock

3 tbsp. soy sauce

1 pinch nutmeg

2 pinches pepper

2 tbsp (rapeseed) oil

Parsley to garnish

Preparation

Heat the oil in a pot and sauté the onion until translucent.

Add the pearl barley and sauté until translucent.

Add the rest of the vegetables and fry briefly.

Add the vegetable stock, bring to a boil and simmer gently for 30 minutes until the pearl barley is cooked.

Sear the smoked tofu in a pan and add to the pot.

Add the spices, bring to a boil and leave to infuse for 5 minutes.

Serve on deep plates sprinkled with parsley.

CHESTNUT CREAM SOUP

Ingredients

400 g chestnuts, coarsely chopped

1000 ml vegetable stock

100 ml vegan white wine

Juice and grated orange

2 onions, diced

1 clove of garlic, pressed

3 tsp fresh thyme

2 tbsp agave syrup

2 pinches pepper

2 tbsp (rapeseed) oil

Preparation

Heat the oil in a pot and fry the onion, garlic, and chestnuts.
Deglaze with agave syrup and white wine and simmer for 5 minutes.
Add the vegetable stock, juice, and zest of the orange and spices.
Simmer gently for 25 minutes until the chestnuts are soft.
Now puree the soup.
Serve on warmed plates.

CELERY - APPLE SOUP

Ingredients

1 small celeriac, finely diced

1 leek, cut into rings

1 onion, diced

1 clove of garlic, pressed

3 apples, variety to taste, peeled, cored, cut into spades.

1000 ml vegetable stock

2 pinches pepper

1 tablespoon lemon juice

100 ml olive oil

Sugar

Cinnamon

some (olive) oil for frying

Preparation

Heat the oil in a pot and sauté the onion, garlic, and leek.
Deglaze with the vegetable stock, add lemon juice, 1 tbsp sugar, and pepper and simmer gently for 15 minutes.
Now puree the soup.
While the soup is cooking, glaze the apple slices in olive oil with a little sugar.
Add the apple slices to the soup and serve dusted with a little cinnamon.

SPICY ORANGE LENTILS SOUP

Ingredients

Juice and grated orange

700 ml vegetable stock

400 ml coconut milk

200 g red lentils, washed and drained

1 onion, diced

1 clove of garlic, pressed

1-2 tsp chili powder (to taste)

2 tsp curry powder

2 pinches pepper

some (rapeseed) oil for frying

Preparation

Heat the oil in a pot and sauté the onion and garlic.
Add the lentils and steam briefly.
Deglaze with the vegetable stock and add the lentils, chili powder, pepper, curry powder, and coconut milk.
Bring to the boil and simmer gently for 25 minutes until the lentils have broken down.
Add the orange juice and the zest.
Now puree the soup and serve on warmed plates.

SWEET POTATO CHICKPEA SOUP

Ingredients

100 g sweet potatoes, diced

240 g chickpeas

200 ml soy cream

1 onion, diced

1 clove of garlic, pressed

400 ml water

1 stock cube

1 tablespoon lemon juice

Pinch of salt

1 tsp pepper

some (rapeseed) oil for sautéing

Preparation

Heat the oil in a pot and sauté the onion with the garlic clove.

Add the sweet potato and sauté.

Add the stock cube and deglaze with 400 ml water.

Add the chickpeas and cook the soup for 20 min.

Then add the soy cream and lemon juice.

Puree the soup well and season with salt and pepper.

CREAM OF MUSHROOM SOUP

Ingredients

100 g mushrooms, sliced

400 ml water

20 ml soy cream

1 stock cube

1 onion, diced

1 clove of garlic, diced

some (rapeseed) oil for sautéing

3 tbsp. flour

½ tsp parsley

1 pinch nutmeg

1 pinch of pepper

some parsley to garnish

Preparation

Heat the oil in a pot and sauté the onion with the garlic clove.

Add the mushrooms and sauté.

Now sweat the flour in the pot.

Add the stock cube and the water.

Simmer the soup for 10 minutes, stirring constantly.

Then puree and refine with pepper and nutmeg.

Finally, add the soy cream and sprinkle with parsley.

POTATO AND LEEK SOUP

Ingredients

700 ml water

1 stock cube

3 potatoes, diced

1 onion, diced

2 leeks, in rings

1 carrot, sliced

50 g ground cashew nuts

3 tbsp. yeast flakes

2 tsp turmeric

1 pinch nutmeg

1 tsp mustard

some (rapeseed) oil for sautéing

some parsley to garnish

Preparation

Heat the oil in the pot and sauté the vegetables in it.

Add the stock cube, cashew nuts, and water and simmer for 15 minutes.

Season to taste with the spices and mustard.

Serve the soup garnished with parsley.

Main dishes

PAPRIKA - COUSCOUS

Ingredients

300 ml vegetable stock

200g couscous

2 peppers

1 tablespoon tomato paste

2 tbsp. soy sauce

2 tbsp curry paste (red or yellow)

2 tbsp white wine vinegar

2 tbsp (olive) oil

Salt, pepper, chili

Preparation

Heat the curry paste with the vegetable stock in a saucepan and bring to a boil.

Add the couscous and remove the pot from the cooker.

Allow the couscous to swell.

Wash, seed, and dice the peppers and add to the couscous later.

Stir together the tomato paste, soy sauce, and vinegar and add to the couscous and pepper mixture.

Add salt, pepper, and chili, and season to taste.

SOUTH TYROLEAN SPINACH DUMPLINGS

Ingredients (6 dumplings)

250 g - 300 g dumpling bread (or bread rolls from the day before)

300 g frozen spinach, drained

3 tbsp soya flour

250ml soy drink

1 onion, diced

1 clove of garlic, pressed

1 tsp salt

2 pinches pepper

20 ml oil

3 tbsp. yeast flakes

Sauce

200 g vegan butter

2 tbsp. yeast flakes

Preparation

Place the dumpling bread in a large bowl (cut the bread into small pieces).

Heat the oil in a pan and sauté the onion and garlic.

Add the spinach and bring to a boil.

Add the soy drink and simmer for 2 minutes over medium heat.

Fold in the soy flour, salt, pepper, and yeast flakes and stir well.

Add everything to the dumpling bread in the bowl and leave to cool slightly.

Mix and form dumplings.

Place the dumplings in a pan of lightly simmering salted water and leave for 20 minutes.

Slowly heat the butter in a saucepan.

When the butter is liquid, add the yeast flakes.

Place the dumplings on a plate and serve with the sauce poured over them.

VEGAN MINCED MEAT STEW

Ingredients

150 g soy granules

2 onions, chopped

2 leeks, in rings

1000 ml vegetable stock

250 ml soy cream

5 tbsp tomato paste

1 tablespoon mustard

1 tsp paprika

1 tsp sugar

1 tsp salt

3 pinches pepper

1 tbsp (rapeseed) oil

Preparation

Prepare the soy granules according to the instructions on the packet. Heat the oil in a pan and fry the onion until translucent.

Add drained soy granules, leek, tomato paste, vegetable stock, mustard, and spices.

Simmer for 15 minutes, stirring several times.

Stir in the soy cream, turn off the heat and leave to infuse for another 5 minutes. Bread can be served as a side dish.

SWEET POTATO PANCAKES

Ingredients (4 large pancakes)

100 g grated sweet potato

100 g wheat flour

1 small onion

200 ml soy drink

2 tbsp soya flour

1 pinch of salt

some (rapeseed) oil for frying

Preparation

Mix the soy flour, soy drink, and flour.
Dice the onion and add it together with the sweet potato and mix well.

Heat the oil in a pan and pour in a quarter of the pancake batter.

Fry for 3 minutes on each side.

TOMATO-LENTIL STEW

Ingredients

2 cans (400g each) of peeled tomatoes

200 g onions

400 g aubergines

250 g red lentils

3 garlic cloves

1 tbsp cumin

5 tbsp olive oil

1 tsp cinnamon

1 red chili pepper

1 tsp sugar

500 ml vegetable stock

2 pinches pepper

3 spring onions

5 stalks parsley

1 tsp lemon juice

possibly a little salt

Preparation

Finely chop the onions and garlic.
Heat two tablespoons of olive oil in a large pot.

Sauté the onions and garlic until translucent.

Add the cinnamon, cumin, and chili pepper and steam briefly.

Add a teaspoon of sugar and let it caramelize slightly.

Add vegetable stock and peeled tomatoes and season with pepper.

Reduce the sauce, uncovered, over medium heat for 20 minutes.

Meanwhile, clean the aubergine and cut it into 2 cm thick cubes.

Heat the remaining olive oil in a pan and fry the aubergine on all sides.

Rinse the lentils in a colander and drain.

Add the lentils to the sauce and cook, covered, for 20 minutes.

Add the aubergines 5 minutes before the end of the cooking time.

Clean the spring onions and cut them into fine rings.

Pluck off the parsley leaves and chop coarsely.

Season the stew with salt, pepper, sugar, and lemon juice.

Serve with spring onions and parsley.

VEGETABLE - COCONUT STEW

Ingredients

200 ml coconut milk

400 g frozen vegetables to taste (carrots, broccoli, etc.)

100 g frozen leaf spinach

300 ml vegetable stock

1 tbsp (rapeseed) oil

2 pinches nutmeg

Salt and pepper to taste

1 tbsp. grated coconut for garnish

Preparation

Bring the vegetable stock to a boil in a large pot and add the frozen vegetables.

Add the oil and nutmeg and simmer for 15 minutes, covered.

Add the coconut milk and bring to a boil briefly.

Season to taste with salt and pepper.

Turn off the heat and let the stew simmer for 5 minutes.

Garnish with grated coconut and serve on deep plates.

PASTA PAN WITH MUSHROOMS

Ingredients

250 g durum wheat spaghetti

1 tsp turmeric

1 onion, diced

3 small courgettes, thinly sliced

250 g mushrooms, sliced

1 tsp cumin

1 tbsp curry powder

4 tbsp. chives or parsley (fresh or frozen)

2 tbsp. soy sauce

(Sesame) oil for frying

Pepper and salt

Preparation

Break (quarter) the spaghetti into four pieces and cook, adding turmeric to the cooking water.

Heat the oil in a pot and sauté the onion.

Add the mushrooms and fry for 3 minutes.

Add the courgettes, cumin, and curry powder and fry for 5 minutes.

Add the spaghetti, soy sauce, pepper, chives/parsley, and mix well.

SMOKED TOFU CASSEROLE

Ingredients

200 g smoked tofu

400 tomato pieces (from the can)

50 ml soy cream

2 onions. diced

3 cloves of garlic, pressed

2 peppers, cut into cubes

1 aubergine, cut into cubes

1 tbsp (rapeseed) oil

1 tsp oregano

Salt and pepper

Preparation

Preheat the oven to a 180° C convection oven.
Heat the oil in a pan and sauté the onion and garlic until translucent.

Add the paprika and steam for 8 minutes over gentle heat.

Put the warm vegetable mixture together with the tofu and aubergine cubes in a shallow baking dish and mix.

Mix the tomatoes with the soy cream and season with pepper, salt, and oregano.

Pour over the casserole and leave to braise in the oven for about 45 minutes.

OVEN VEGETABLES

Ingredients

4 potatoes

1 courgette

2 peppers

2 onions

4 tbsp olive oil

1 - 2 tbsp. spices to taste (rosemary, thyme, oregano...)

Salt and pepper to taste

Preparation

Preheat the oven to a 180° C convection oven.

Cut the potatoes into wedges. Cut the courgettes into slices. Cut the peppers into strips. Cut onion into rings.

Line a baking tray with baking paper and spread the vegetables evenly on it.

Sprinkle the spices over the vegetables.

Cook in the oven for 30 - 35 minutes.

Leave to cool briefly and serve.

SPINACH - RISOTTO

Ingredients

300 g risotto rice

400 g fresh baby spinach, cut (or frozen spinach, drained)

1 red chili pepper, deseeded and finely chopped

2 stalks of lemongrass, make a knot from each stalk.

1 onion, chopped

2 cloves of garlic, pressed

1200 ml vegetable stock

300 ml vegan white wine

1 tablespoon lemon juice

some salt and pepper

2 tbsp (olive) oil

Preparation

Heat the oil in a pot and sauté the onion and garlic.
Add the rice and stir well.

After 1 minute, add white wine and simmer.

Add the lemongrass knots, then gradually add the vegetable stock and cook the risotto for 15 minutes, stirring constantly.

Remove the lemongrass and add the spinach leaves.

Simmer for a further 5 minutes, stirring constantly. (Until the spinach has collapsed).

Season with lemon juice, salt, and pepper.

PUMPKIN RAGOUT

Ingredients

½ Hokkaido pumpkin

250 ml soy drink

2 tbsp flour

1 tbsp. yeast flakes

1 pinch nutmeg

2 tbsp (rapeseed) oil

Salt

Preparation

Cut the washed and cored pumpkin into pieces of about 2x2 centimeters.

Heat the oil in a saucepan and sauté the pumpkin.

Stir in the flour until it has combined with the oil.

Slowly add the vegetable drink. Stir diligently so that no lumps form.

Add the yeast flakes and season with salt and nutmeg.

Simmer on low for 15 minutes, stirring occasionally, until the pumpkin cubes are soft.

BAKED APPLE STRUDEL WITH VANILLA SAUCE

Ingredients

For the dough

250 g flour

100 ml lukewarm water

1 tsp locust bean gum

1 pinch of salt

For the filling

1200 g apples, peeled and cored

50 g marzipan paste

5 tbsp. lemon juice

3 tbsp almond slivers

1 tsp cinnamon

2 tablespoons orange juice

Vanilla sauce

600 ml vanilla-flavored vegetable drink

3 tbsp cornflour

Preparation

For the dough, knead all the ingredients, adding the water slowly to make a firm, elastic dough.

Wrap in cling film and leave to rest for an hour.

Preheat the oven to 180°C.

Quarter 400 g of the apple and place it on a baking tray lined with baking paper. And brush with a little lemon juice, and sprinkle with almonds and marzipan.

Bake in the oven for 12 minutes.

Finely slice the remaining apples and mix with the remaining lemon juice and cinnamon and leave to infuse.

Roll out the dough into a rectangle and spread it out on a large kitchen towel and dust well with flour.

Roll out the dough so thinly that the pattern of the cloth shows through.

Lightly mash the baked apples together with the marzipan and almonds with a fork and mix with the marinated apples.

Spread the apple mixture evenly over the pastry, leaving a 3 cm border.

Fold in the "short" sides of the pastry rectangle up to the filling.

Roll up from the long side using the kitchen towel.

Now place the strudel on the tray with the help of the kitchen towel so that the seam is at the bottom.

Bake in the oven for 45 minutes.

For the custard, take a few spoonfuls of the soy milk and mix with the cornflour.

Bring the remaining soy milk to the boil, stir in the mixed powder and bring to the boil again briefly.

LENTIL-PARANUT ROAST

Ingredients

250 g red lentils

300 g Brazil nuts

400 ml water

1 onion

120 g breadcrumbs

2 garlic cloves

1 carrot

1 bay leaf

1 tbsp. soy sauce

1 tablespoon tomato paste

1 tablespoon oregano

2 tbsp (rapeseed) oil for frying

some vegan butter for greasing

Side dish: Rice

Preparation

Preheat the oven to 180 °C.

Bring the lentils and bay leaf to a boil in a pot with 400 ml of water.

Cook for 25 minutes.

Remove the bay leaf and set the lentils aside.

Heat the oil in a pan.

Sauté the chopped onion, pressed garlic cloves, and chopped carrot for 3 minutes.

Coarsely chop one-third of the Brazil nuts. Finely grind the remaining Brazil nuts.

Place the sautéed onion mixture in a bowl with the ground and chopped Brazil nuts.

Add the lentils, breadcrumbs, tomato paste, soy sauce, and oregano and mix well.

Place in a baking dish greased with butter.

Bake in the oven for 25 minutes.

Leave to cool a little.

Remove carefully and serve with rice.

COCONUT SPAGHETTI

Ingredients

500 g spaghetti

600 ml coconut milk

700 ml vegetable stock

4 peppers

4 carrots

2 onions

2 tbsp curry

Pepper and salt to taste

Preparation

Cut the peppers and carrots into small cubes.

Put all the ingredients, except the spaghetti, in a saucepan and bring to a boil.

Simmer on medium heat for 5 minutes.

Add the spaghetti and cook according to the instructions on the packet until al dente.

Season to taste with salt and pepper.

BAKED BEANS

Ingredients

2 cans of white beans

400 g strained tomatoes

3 tbsp tomato paste

1 onion

1 clove of garlic

3 tablespoons sugar

1 tbsp (rapeseed) oil

Salt

Pepper

Chilli powder

Preparation

Preheat the oven to a 180 C convection oven.
Press the garlic clove and chop the onion.

Heat the oil in a pan and fry the onion and garlic until translucent.

Place the beans with the strained tomatoes in a casserole dish.

Add the sautéed onion with the garlic and the remaining ingredients to the casserole dish and mix everything well.

Bake in the oven for 30 minutes.

WINTER RATATOUILLE

Ingredients

1 can (400 g each) peeled tomatoes

4 carrots

100 ml water

150 g aubergine

100 g couscous

1 clove of garlic

2 tbsp (rapeseed) oil

1 tsp curry powder

1 pinch of sugar

Some salt

Preparation

Clean the aubergine and dice 1.5 cm.
Heat a tsp of oil in a large, coated frying pan.

Fry the aubergine in it until light brown and season with salt.

Meanwhile, peel and slice 4 carrots.

Put the aubergine on a plate.

Sauté the carrots in the pan with 1 tsp oil.

Finely chop the garlic clove, add with the curry powder, and steam briefly.

Add the tomatoes and 100 ml water, bring to a boil, and season with salt and 1 pinch of sugar.

Cook over a gentle heat for 10 minutes.

Pour 150 ml boiling water over the couscous with a little salt in a bowl.

Cover and leave to soak for at least 5 minutes.

Mix the aubergines into the sauce.

Heat briefly and serve with couscous.

PICHELSTEINER

Ingredients

40 g soy cubes (dry product)

400 g potato, sliced

200 g kohlrabi, sliced

200 g carrots, sliced

200 g celery, sliced or diced

1 leek, in rings

1 onion, chopped

3 tbsp (rapeseed) oil

1000 ml vegetable stock

Salt, pepper, and nutmeg

4 tbsp parsley to garnish

Preparation

Bring the soy cubes to a boil in the vegetable stock and leave to infuse for 10 minutes. Remove the soy cubes from the vegetable broth with a sieve.

Set aside the vegetable stock.

Heat the oil in a pot and add the onion, leek, potato, kohlrabi, celery, carrots, and soy cubes in layers.

Season each layer lightly with salt, pepper, and nutmeg.

Pour over vegetable stock until the vegetables are ¾ covered.

Cover and simmer for 30 minutes over medium heat. Do not stir! When the potatoes are firm to the bite, stir and serve garnished with parsley.

GRILLED CORN ON THE COB

Ingredients

4 corn on the cob

50 g vegan butter

1 tablespoon herb mixture to taste

Some (rapeseed) oil

Preparation

Pre-cook the corn on the cob for about 15 minutes and leave it to cool slightly.

Preheat the grill and brush the grate with oil.

Pierce the corn on the cob lengthwise with a barbecue skewer and brush with a little butter and season with herb mix.

Place the corn on the cobs on the grill and grill evenly for about 10 minutes.

CHICKPEA CURRY

Ingredients

1 tin chickpeas (400 g)

1 can coconut milk (400 ml)

100 ml vegan white wine

1 onion, finely chopped

2 cloves of garlic, pressed

2 tbsp. yeast flakes

2 tbsp curry

1 tbsp. soy sauce

1 tsp sugar

3 tbsp (rapeseed) oil

Side dish: Rice

Preparation

Heat the oil in a pot and sauté the onion and garlic until translucent.

Deglaze with white wine and simmer a little.

Slowly stir in the coconut milk.

Add curry, yeast flakes, soy sauce, sugar, and chickpeas.

Simmer on medium heat for 10 minutes.

Serve the chickpea curry with rice.

POTATO GOULASH

Ingredients

250 g mushrooms, in pieces

2 potatoes, diced

1 onion, finely chopped

2 cloves of garlic, pressed

2 red peppers, diced

2 tsp tomato paste

1 tsp caraway

1 tsp marjoram

1 tsp salt and 1 tsp pepper

2 tsp paprika

3 pinches of chili powder

4 tbsp (rapeseed) oil for frying

Water to cover the potatoes

Preparation

Heat 2 tbsp oil in a large saucepan and fry the onion until translucent.

Add the tomato paste, potato, paprika, and garlic.

After 3 minutes, add water so that the potatoes are covered.

Add the remaining ingredients and simmer for 10 minutes until soft.

Heat the remaining oil in a pan and fry the mushrooms until golden brown.

Stir in the mushrooms and serve on warmed plates.

POTATO - CARROT RÖSTI

Ingredients (8 Rösti)

200 g potatoes

200 g carrots

2 tablespoons soy drink

1 tablespoon cornflour

½ tsp lemon juice

Pinch of nutmeg

3 tbsp (rapeseed) oil

Salt

Preparation

Peel the potatoes and carrots and grate them coarsely with a kitchen grater.

Mix with soy drink, cornflour, lemon juice, salt, and nutmeg.

Heat the oil in a pan.

Using round cutters, form 8 equally sized rösti in the pan.

Remove the cutters and allow the rösti to fry on both sides until nice and golden brown.

KOHLRABI POTATO VEGETABLES

Ingredients

1 kg kohlrabi

2 carrots

2 potatoes

100 ml soy cream

1 tsp salt

3 pinches pepper

3 pinches nutmeg

1 tsp vegetable stock

3 tbsp vegan butter

Boiling water

Preparation

Cut the kohlrabi, potatoes, and carrots into cubes.

Cook the vegetables with the salt in a pot of water until soft.

Pour off the water.

Mix with remaining ingredients and puree.

GRILLED PEPPER SKEWERS

Ingredients

1 each of red, yellow, orange, and green peppers.
10 rosemary sprigs
1 tbsp garlic powder
2 tbsp agave syrup
250 ml olive oil
Salt and pepper

Preparation

Cut the peppers into bite-sized pieces and stick them on the rosemary sprigs.

Mix the olive oil, agave syrup, salt, pepper, and garlic powder, and marinate the pepper skewers in it for 30 minutes.

Preheat the grill and brush the grate with oil.

Grill the pepper skewers for approx. 12 minutes, turning regularly.

SPAGHETTI WITH PEANUT SAUCE

Ingredients

300 g spaghetti

800 ml vegetable stock

120 g roasted peanuts

1 pepper, finely diced

1 carrot, finely diced

3 onions, finely chopped

3 cloves of garlic, pressed

1 piece ginger

1 tablespoon sugar

2 tablespoons lemon juice

2 tbsp peanut butter

1 tsp coriander

1 tablespoon soy sauce

2 tbsp (olive) oil for frying

Preparation

Heat the oil in a saucepan and fry the onion and garlic until translucent.

Add all ingredients except lemon juice and coriander and simmer until the spaghetti is al dente.

Add the coriander and lemon juice.
Mix well again and serve.

GRILLED MUSHROOM SKEWERS

Ingredients

500 g cleaned mushrooms

4 cloves of pressed garlic

4 tbsp. soy sauce

2 tbsp agave syrup

1 tsp oregano

1 tsp thyme

2 tbsp olive oil

½ tsp pepper

Preparation

Preheat the grill and brush the grate with oil.

Mix the garlic with the oil, soy sauce, pepper, agave syrup, oregano, and thyme to make a marinade Add the mushrooms to the marinade.

Distribute the mushrooms on skewers and place them on the grill.

Grill until done, turning regularly.

FRIED TOFU

Ingredients

400 g tofu

400 ml coconut milk

60 g ginger

2 Garlic

1 lime

2 tsp sugar

2 tsp paprika

½ tsp salt

3 tbsp (rapeseed) oil

Preparation

Cut the tofu into pieces about 1 cm wide and 4 cm long.

Chop the ginger and garlic cloves.

Mix with coconut milk, juice of 1 lime, sugar, paprika, and salt.

Place the tofu in the marinade and leave to marinate for at least 2 hours.

Remove the tofu from the marinade and pat dry.

Heat the oil in a pan and fry the tofu for 5 minutes.

Sweets - Cookies

WAFFLES

Ingredients

120 g vegan butter

1 tsp sugar

25 ml water

250 ml soy drink

250 g flour

25 g apple puree

2 tsp soya flour

½ tsp baking powder

Preparation

Mix the sugar and butter in a bowl.

Add the applesauce, flour, and soy flour and mix again.

Add the baking powder, soy drink, and water and mix well.

Mix the dough with the mixer so that it is creamy and smooth.

Bake the batter in the waffle iron.

Top the finished waffles as desired.

MARZIPAN POTATOES

Ingredients (50 potatoes)

For the dough

200 g marzipan paste

200 g icing sugar

1 tsp water

1 pinch of salt

For decorating

2 tbsp cocoa powder

1 pinch cinnamon

Preparation

Warm the marzipan slightly.

Knead with the icing sugar, salt, and water.

Shape the marzipan into cherry-sized balls.

Sieve the cocoa with the cinnamon onto a plate and roll the marzipan balls in it.

Place the balls in a fine sieve and shake briefly to shake off the excess cocoa powder.

MOCHA COOKIES

Ingredients (15 pieces)

130 g sugar

130 g vegan butter

130 g flour

½ tsp baking powder

1 tablespoon instant espresso powder

50 g fine oat flakes

1 pinch of salt

Preparation

Preheat the oven to 180°C.

Mix the flour, sugar, baking powder, and cocoa.

Dissolve the espresso powder in 1 tbsp boiling water and stir in.

Add the butter and oat flakes and work into a soft dough.

Form 15 balls and press them a little flat on a baking tray lined with baking paper. Make sure there is a little space between them.

Bake in the oven for 15 minutes

CINNAMON STARS

Ingredients (about 50 stars)

For the biscuit dough

200 g icing sugar

2 tablespoons cinnamon

8 tbsp. water

1 tablespoon lemon juice

200 g ground hazelnuts

200 g ground almonds

1 tbsp grated orange zest

1 pinch of salt

Flour for the work surface

For the cast

150 g icing sugar

Some water

1 tsp cinnamon

Preparation

Preheat the oven to 180°C.

Mix all the ingredients except the flour.

Dust the work surface with flour. If the dough is too sticky, simply add some more flour.

Roll out the dough to about 1 cm thick.

Cut out stars with the biscuit cutter and place them on a baking tray lined with baking paper.

Bake the cinnamon stars in the preheated oven for about 7 minutes.

Place the still soft cinnamon stars on a wire rack to cool.

For the icing, simply mix all the ingredients and brush the stars with it.

NUT BISCUITS

Ingredients (about 40 biscuits)

For the dough

300 g flour

2 sachets custard powder

100 g tender oat flakes

150 g ground hazelnuts

120 g sugar

½ packet of baking powder

200 g vegan butter

½ tsp cinnamon

6 tbsp. water

some icing sugar for decorating

To coat

100 g sour cherry jam

Preparation

For the dough, first, mix all the dry ingredients in a bowl.

Knead with butter and water to form a shortcrust pastry.

If necessary, add a little water or flour until the dough is no longer sticky but can be kneaded well.

Place the dough in the fridge for 30 minutes.

Preheat the oven to 180°C.

Roll out the dough in portions on the floured work surface to a thickness of 5 mm and cut out using cookie cutters.

Bake in the oven for 15 minutes.

Leave the biscuits to cool.

In the meantime, heat the sour cherry jam and pass it through a sieve.

Spread half of the biscuits with the jam and place a dry biscuit on top.

Finally, dust with icing sugar.

MARZIPAN NOUGAT PRALINES

Ingredients

For the dough

200 g marzipan paste

150 g icing sugar

175 g vegan nougat

1 pinch of salt

For decorating

50 g coarsely chopped pistachio kernels

200 g vegan dark chocolate

Preparation

Warm the marzipan slightly.

Knead with icing sugar.

Roll out the marzipan between two layers of baking paper to a rectangle 5mm thick.

Heat the nougat over a water bath until it becomes spreadable.

Spread evenly over the marzipan.

Roll up the marzipan sheet from the long side into a roll.

Place cling film in the fridge for 2 hours.

Melt the dark chocolate.

In the meantime, cut bite-sized pieces from the marzipan roll and shape them into a praline ball.

Dip this marzipan nougat praline into the chocolate.

Sprinkle the top with pistachios and leave to cool.

COCONUT MACAROONS

Ingredients (40 pieces)

180 g sugar

1 tsp lemon juice

200 g grated coconut

Aquafaba (use the drained water from a 400 ml can of chickpeas)

½ tsp baking powder

(Optional baking wafers)

Preparation

Preheat the oven to 180°C.

Line two baking trays with baking paper.

Beat the aquafaba with the lemon juice and baking powder until stiff.

Add the grated coconut and mix well.

Take small portions with a teaspoon and place them on the baking paper.

(Optionally place on round baking wafers)

Bake the coconut macaroons in the preheated oven for about 18 minutes until they turn slightly golden brown.

Leave to cool on a cooling rack.

CHOCOLATE PRALINES

Ingredients (50 chocolates)

For the dough

200 g vegan dark chocolate

60 g ground almonds

80 g soy cream

4 tbsp. orange juice

1 tsp grated orange zest

1 pinch of salt

For decorating

300 g vegan dark chocolate

Preparation

Heat the soy cream and dissolve 200 g of chocolate in it.

Stir in the orange juice, grated orange zest, and almonds.

Leave to cool in the fridge for 5 hours.

Grate 100g chocolate.

Melt 200g chocolate.

Cover the balls with liquid chocolate.

Put the grated chocolate in a small bowl and roll the balls in it.

SPECULOOS

Ingredients (10 speculoos)

200 g flour

100 g vegan butter

80 g sugar

1 pinch of salt

1 tablespoon soy drink

2 tbsp gingerbread spice

Preparation

Mix the flour, sugar, salt, and gingerbread spice.
Add the butter and soy drink and knead it into a dough.

Leave the dough to rest in the fridge for 30 minutes, wrapped in cling film.

On a floured work surface, roll out the dough to about 5 mm thick.

Preheat the oven to 180°C.

Using a pizza cutter and a ruler, cut the dough into even rectangles.

Decorate rectangles with patterns as desired.

Carefully lift the speculoos and place them on a baking tray lined with baking paper.

Bake in the oven for 8 minutes.

GINGERBREAD

Ingredients (40 gingerbread)

Mix 3 tbsp soy flour with 90 ml of water

90 g brown sugar

1 tbsp agave syrup

1 ½ tsp cinnamon, ground

¼ tsp ginger, ground

¼ tsp mace, ground

1 pinch cardamom, ground

¼ tsp nutmeg, ground

¼ tsp clove, ground

1 pinch of salt

125 g ground almonds

125 g ground hazelnuts

100 g candied lemon peel

100 g candied orange peel

1 pack of wafers, 40mm

For the cast

100 g icing sugar

3 tbsp. lemon juice

Preparation

Preheat the oven to 160°C top/bottom heat.

Mix the soy flour with the water and leave it to stand for a short time.

Add all the other ingredients and mix.

Shape a tablespoon of sticky dough into a ball with moistened hands and press it into a wafer. The wafer should be completely covered.

Place the gingerbread on a baking tray lined with baking paper and bake for 15 minutes in a preheated oven at 160°C.

Leave the baked gingerbread to cool.

Mix the icing sugar with the lemon juice and coat the gingerbread with the icing.

Optionally decorate with almonds, sultanas, or other nuts.

CHRISTSTOLLEN

Ingredients

500 g flour

1 sachet of dry yeast

130 g sugar

1 pinch of salt

1 tablespoon lemon zest

200 g vegan butter

250 ml soy drink

150 g sultanas

100 g ground almonds

100 g marzipan

some icing sugar

2 tbsp vegan butter

Preparation

Mix all the ingredients (except the sultanas and marzipan) together and knead them into a dough.

Leave the dough to rise in a warm place for 2 hours.

Preheat the oven to 180°C.

Pull the dough apart a little, sprinkle the sultanas on top, and knead the dough into a ball again.

Then roll out the dough into a rectangle (approx. 30 x 25 cm) and roll up from the longer side.

Shape the marzipan into a sausage shape, approximately the length of the pastry.

Bake the stollen for 15 minutes.

Reduce the temperature to 160°C and bake for a further 45 minutes.

After cooling, brush the Christstollen with 2 tbsp melted margarine.

Sprinkle with plenty of icing sugar and serve.

SWEET SHORTBREAD COOKIES

Ingredients (40 biscuits)

For the dough

100 g icing sugar

200 g vegan butter

350 g flour

1 tbsp soy flour, mixed in 30 ml water

1 pinch of salt

1 sachet of vanilla sugar

some flour for the work surface

For decorating

150 g icing sugar

Some water

Sugar/chocolate sprinkles

Preparation

Put all the ingredients in a bowl and knead together.

Wrap the dough in cling film and leave it to rest in the fridge for an hour.

Preheat the oven to 180°C.

Roll out the dough with a rolling pin on the floured work surface to a thickness of 5 mm.

Cut out biscuits with biscuit cutters and place them on a baking tray lined with baking paper.

Bake the biscuits in the preheated oven for about 10 minutes until golden.

Leave to cool on a cooling rack.

For the icing, simply mix the icing sugar with a little water.

Coat the biscuits with the icing and decorate with sprinkles.

To store, it is best to put them in a biscuit tin.

CINNAMON MUFFINS

Ingredients (12 muffins)

For the dough

100 g tender oat flakes

250 ml soy drink

80 g vegan butter

400 g flour

1 sachet of vanilla sugar

40 g yeast (1 packet dry yeast)

For the filling

50 g vegan butter

4 tbsp agave syrup

1 tablespoon cinnamon

Preparation

Mix all the ingredients and knead them into a dough.

Leave to rise in a warm place for one hour.

Roll out the dough into a rectangle on the floured work surface.

For the filling, melt the butter, with agave syrup.

Coat the pastry with the mixture and dust with cinnamon.

Roll up the rectangle and cut 2cm thick slices.

Place each one in a muffin tin and leave to rise for another 20 minutes.

Preheat the oven to 180°C. Bake in the oven for 12 minutes.

BUTTER BISCUITS

Ingredients (30 pieces)

100 g sugar

1 tbsp soy flour, mixed in 30 ml water

100 g vegan butter

250 g flour

1 tsp baking powder

some sugar for decoration

Preparation

Preheat the oven to 180°C.

Knead all the ingredients into a dough.

Put some sugar on a plate.

Shape a tablespoon of dough into a ball and press one side into the sugar.

Place the balls, sugared side up, on a baking tray lined with baking paper.

Bake the biscuits in the preheated oven for about 20 minutes until golden.

Leave to cool on a cooling rack.

CARDAMOM BISCUITS

Ingredients (50 pieces)

For the dough

100 g sugar

200 g vegan butter

250 g flour

6 tbsp orange juice

½ tsp baking powder

1 tsp ground cardamom

For the topping

150 roasted macadamia nuts

Preparation

Preheat the oven to 180°C.

Mix all the ingredients.

Place the batter in a piping bag and pipe dots onto a baking tray lined with baking paper.

Rinse the roasted macadamia nuts.

Place one still wet nut on each dab.

Bake in the oven for 10 minutes.

VANILLA CRESCENT COOKIES

Ingredients (30 pieces)

For the dough

200 g flour

100 g ground almonds

200 g vegan butter

160 g sugar

1 sachet custard powder

1 sachet of vanilla sugar

1 tsp baking powder

2 tablespoons water

For garnishing

2 tbsp icing sugar and 1 sachet of vanilla sugar

Preparation

Preheat the oven to 180°C.

Mix all the dry ingredients in a bowl.

Knead with butter and water to a smooth dough.

Place the dough in the fridge for 30 minutes.

Then form the dough in portions into 2 cm thick rolls.

Cut the rolls into pieces about 6 cm long.

Bend the pieces into croissants, place them on a baking tray lined with baking paper and flatten slightly. Bake in the oven for 12 minutes.

While still warm, dust with the mixture of icing sugar and vanilla sugar.

BANANA CINNAMON COOKIES

Ingredients (40 pieces)

300 g flour

50 g ground almonds

100 g vegan butter

100 g sugar

1 banana

2 tablespoons cinnamon

1 tsp baking powder

2 tablespoons soy drink

Preparation

Mash the banana and knead it into a dough with all the ingredients.

Leave the dough to rise for 10 minutes.

Preheat the oven to 180°C.

Roll out the dough and cut out biscuits with biscuit cutters.

Place the biscuits on a baking tray lined with baking paper.

Bake in the oven for 15 minutes.

ORANGENTALER

Ingredients (40 pieces)

For the dough

200 g flour

100 g ground almonds

200 g vegan butter

150 g sugar

1 sachet custard powder

½ grated orange zest

75 g chopped dark chocolate

1 tsp baking powder

2 tablespoons orange juice

For garnishing

75 g sugar

Preparation

Mix all the dry ingredients in a bowl.

Knead with butter and orange juice until smooth.

Place the dough in the fridge for 30 minutes.

Preheat the oven to 180°C.

Form the dough in portions into a 4 cm thick roll.

Roll the rolls in sugar and cut them into 5 mm thick slices.

Bend the pieces into croissants and place them on a baking tray lined with baking paper. Bake in the oven for 10 minutes.

LINZ EYES

Ingredients (80 pieces)

300 g flour

200 g vegan butter

110 g icing sugar

80 g ground almonds

5 tbsp. soy drink

1 tsp vanilla sugar

grated zest of half a lemon

1 pinch cinnamon

150 g jam for filling

Preparation

Mix all the dry ingredients in a bowl.

Add the soy drink and margarine to the flour mixture in batches.

Mix all ingredients well and knead into a dough.

Cover the dough airtight and let it rest in the refrigerator for one hour.

Preheat the oven to 180 °C.

Then knead the dough again.

Roll out the dough to a thickness of four millimeters on a floured work surface.

Cut out biscuits with biscuit cutters (the biscuit cutters must be large enough so that you can still poke one or two holes in the biscuit).

Cut out small holes in half of the vegan biscuits - the jam will show through here later.

Place the biscuits on a baking tray lined with baking paper and bake in the preheated oven for 8 minutes until golden.

Leave the biscuits to cool.

Stir the jam until smooth and spread it on the biscuit halves without the hole.

Put the Linz eyes together.

MARBLE BISCUITS

Ingredients (50 pieces)

300 g flour

200 g vegan butter

130 g sugar

1 tbsp. vanilla custard powder

1 tsp baking powder

2 tbsp cocoa powder

2 tablespoons water

Preparation

Knead all ingredients, except cocoa powder, into a shortcrust pastry.

Divide the dough in half and knead one half with cocoa powder.

If the dough is dry, add a little more water.

Roughly knead both halves of the dough together to create a nice grain.

Wrap the dough in cling film and place it in the fridge for one hour.

Preheat the oven to 180°C.

Shape the dough in portions into rolls of approx. 4 cm diameter.

Cut slices approx. 1 cm thick with a sharp knife.

Place the slices on a baking tray lined with baking paper.

Bake in the oven for 12 minutes.

LEMON BISCUITS

Ingredients (50 pieces)

230 g flour

120 g vegan butter

130 g sugar

1 tbsp soy flour and 1 tbsp water mixed

Grated lemon and juice of one lemon

Preparation

Knead all the ingredients into a dough.

Shape the dough into a ball and place it in the fridge for one hour.

Preheat the oven to 180°C.

Roll out the dough on a floured work surface to a thickness of 1 cm and cut out the biscuits with biscuit cutters.

Place the biscuits on a baking tray lined with baking paper.

Bake in the oven for about 10 minutes.

OAT BISCUITS

Ingredients (30 pieces)

100 g vegan butter

120 g seeded oat flakes

100 g flour

120 g sugar

1 sachet of vanilla sugar

½ teaspoon baking powder

50 g chopped almonds

Preparation

Preheat the oven to 180°C.

Melt the butter for the dough.

Stir in the oat flakes and leave to cool slightly.

Add the remaining ingredients and knead into a soft dough.

Using two teaspoons, place small portions on a baking tray lined with baking paper and flatten them slightly.

Bake in the oven for 15 minutes.

SHORTBREAD BISCUITS

Ingredients (70 pieces)

For the dough

120 g sugar

60 g ground almonds

190 g vegan butter, room temperature

250 g flour

1 sachet of vanilla sugar

50 g soy drink

1 pinch of salt

For decorating

melted dark chocolate coating

Preparation

Mix the sugar, butter, salt, and soy drink.

Add the almonds and flour and knead well.

Preheat the oven to 180°C.

Using a pastry press or piping bag, pipe bars, rings, S-shapes, etc., and place on a baking tray lined with baking paper.

Bake the biscuits in the preheated oven for about 12 minutes until light yellow.

Leave to cool on a cooling rack.

Spread half of the biscuit with melted dark chocolate.

MINI ALMOND CORNERS

Ingredients (70 pieces)

For the dough

200 g vegan butter

400 g flour

100 g sugar

2 tablespoons soy drink

half a bottle of almond flavoring

For the topping

50 g candied orange peel

200 g chopped almonds

50 g sliced almonds

100 g ground almonds

80 g sugar

100 g vegan butter

200 ml soy drink

Additionally

80 g apricot jam

150 g vegan dark chocolate

Preparation

Preheat the oven to 180°C.

Mix all the ingredients for the dough.

Wrap the dough in cling film and leave it to rest in the fridge for 30 minutes.

Roll out the dough thinly on a baking tray lined with baking paper.

Spread the apricot jam evenly on top.

Chop the candied orange peel.

Toast the candied orange peel, the chopped, and the sliced almonds in a well-heated pan until golden brown, stirring frequently.

Add the ground almonds, sugar, and butter. Stir and turn off the cooker.

Stir in the soy drink.

Pour this nut mixture onto the prepared dough and spread evenly.

Bake in the oven for 25 minutes.

Leave to cool and cut into even squares.

Then, using a sharp knife, divide the squares crosswise to create almond corners.

Brush the corners of the almonds with melted dark chocolate and allow the chocolate to harden.

Cake

CHOCOLATE CAKE

Ingredients

For the dough

130 ml oil

250 g sugar

300 g flour

125 g chopped dark chocolate

1 sachet of baking powder

350 ml soy drink

4 tablespoons rum

2 tsp locust bean gum

For the decoration

150 g dark chocolate

2 tbsp icing sugar

Preparation

Preheat the oven to 180°C.

For the dough, mix all the dry ingredients in a bowl.

Add the soy drink, rum, and oil and mix, e.g. with a hand mixer, until smooth.

Pour the batter into a springform pan lined with baking paper.

Bake in the oven for 45 minutes.

APPLE TART

Ingredients

For the dough

80 g vegan butter, a little more for greasing

250 g sugar

150 g flour, a little more for flouring

50 ml water

1 tsp vanilla sugar

For the topping

1 kg apples

40 g sugar

10 g vegan butter

Preparation

Preheat the oven to 180°C.

Grease and flour the tart tin (Ø 26cm).

Mix all the dough ingredients in a bowl and knead them into a dough.

Roll out the dough on a lightly floured work surface and line the tart tin with it.

Peel and core the apples cut them into thin slices and spread them like a fan on the pastry.

Sprinkle with sugar and spread the butter on top.

Bake in the oven for 35 minutes.

CARROT CAKE

Ingredients

250 g carrots

200 g ground nuts (to taste)

1 Apple

130 g flour

100 g sugar

1 package of baking powder

1 tsp cinnamon

½ tsp cardamom

130 ml soy drink

100 ml (rapeseed) oil

For the glaze:

Mix 100 g icing sugar with 2 tbsp lemon juice

Preparation

Preheat the oven to 180°C.

Mix all dry ingredients incl. spices.

Add the soy drink and oil and mix quickly with the dry ingredients.

Finely grate the carrots and apple and fold them in.

Pour the dough into a greased springform pan lined with baking paper and bake in the oven for approx. 45 minutes.

After cooling, coat with the icing sugar glaze.

ALMOND CAKE

Ingredients

For the dough

100 g sugar

200 g vegan butter

300 g flour

1 tbsp. vanilla custard powder

1 sachet of vanilla sugar

6 tbsp agave syrup

2 tablespoons water

For the filling

200 g almonds

120 g icing sugar

1 sachet of vanilla sugar

2 tablespoons water

1 tbsp agave syrup

Preparation

For the dough, first, mix all the dry ingredients in a bowl.

Knead with butter, agave syrup, and water to form a shortcrust pastry.

If necessary, add a little water or flour until the dough is no longer sticky but can be kneaded well.

Put the dough in the fridge for an hour.

Preheat the oven to 180°C

For the filling, heat all the ingredients in a saucepan, but do not boil.

Allow cooling.

Line the base of a springform pan lined with baking paper with half of the dough and draw a rim about 1.5 cm high.

Spread the almond mixture over the pastry base.

Roll out the rest of the pastry and place it over the filling as a lid.

Prick several times with a fork.

Bake in the oven for 35 minutes.

WALNUT CAKE

Ingredients

100 g vegan butter

250 g sugar

4 tbsp soya flour

250 g flour

150 g finely chopped walnuts

2 tsp baking powder

250 ml soy drink

Couverture

chopped walnuts

Preparation

Preheat the oven to 180°C.

Beat the butter and sugar until fluffy. Stir in the soy flour.

Mix the flour, finely chopped walnuts, and baking powder and stir in alternately with the soy drink.

Pour the dough into a greased springform pan and bake for 40-50 minutes. Leave the cake to cool.

Melt the couverture and coat the cake with it.

Decorate with a few walnuts.

BUNDT CAKE

Ingredients

For the dough

400 g sugar

some butter for greasing

350 g flour and a little more to flour a springform pan

2 tsp baking powder

1 tsp bicarbonate of soda

1 sachet of vanilla sugar

60 g grated coconut

500 ml soy drink

250 g berries of your choice with 1 tsp salt

For decorating

Icing sugar for dusting

Preparation

Preheat the oven to 180°C.

Grease and flour a 24 cm cupcake tin with butter.

Mix the baking powder, baking soda, flour, vanilla sugar, sugar, and grated coconut.

Add the soy drink and oil and mix until smooth.

Fold in the salt and berries.

Pour the batter into the springform pan and bake in the oven for 60 minutes. Leave to cool slightly and turn out onto a cake rack.

Dust cooled cupcakes with icing sugar.

CARROT CAKE

Ingredients

250 g carrots

200 g ground nuts (to taste)

1 Apple

130 g flour

100 g sugar

1 package of baking powder

1 tsp cinnamon

½ tsp cardamom

130 ml soy drink

100 ml (rapeseed) oil

For the glaze:

Mix 100 g icing sugar with 2 tbsp lemon juice

Preparation

Preheat the oven to 180°C.

Mix all dry ingredients incl. spices.

Add the soy drink and oil and mix quickly with the dry ingredients.

Finely grate the carrots and apple and fold them in.

Pour the dough into a greased springform pan lined with baking paper and bake in the oven for approx. 45 minutes.

After cooling, coat with the icing sugar glaze.

Desserts

PEAR WITH CARAMEL SAUCE

Ingredients (4 servings)

For the pears

4 pears

100 ml white port wine

400 ml white wine

50 g sugar

1 tablespoon cinnamon

1 sachet of vanilla sugar

For the caramel sauce

100 ml boiling water

60 g sugar

Preparation

Peel the pears and carefully cut out the core.

Bring all the ingredients to a boil in the saucepan.

Add the peas and simmer for 4 minutes.

Cover the pot and leave to cool.

For the caramel sauce, caramelize the sugar in a saucepan and deglaze with 100 ml of boiling water.

Remove the pears from the wine broth and place them on a plate.

Pour over the caramel sauce and serve.

Sieve wine stock. Can be used as a drink with this.

CHOCOLATE MOUSSE

Ingredients (4 servings)

250 g silken tofu

150 g vegan chocolate

1 tbsp vegan rum

1 sachet of vanilla sugar

1 tablespoon sugar

Fruits for garnishing

Preparation

Puree silken tofu

Melt the chocolate in a hot water bath.

Mix all the ingredients except the fruit and fill them into glasses.

Chill in the fridge for at least 3 hours.

Serve garnished with fresh fruit.

MULLED WINE CHERRY GINGERBREAD MOUSSE

Ingredients (4 servings)

For the mousse

400 g silken tofu

200 g dark chocolate

3 packets of vanilla sugar

1 tbsp gingerbread spice

5 tbsp. soy drink

3 tbsp boiled espresso

For the mulled wine cherries

200 g morello cherries

200 ml mulled wine

1 tsp cinnamon

3 tbsp agave syrup

1 tablespoon cornflour

Preparation

Melt the chocolate with the espresso over a water bath.

Puree the silken tofu with the soy drink, gingerbread spice, and vanilla sugar.

Mix everything and put it in the fridge.

Drain the morello cherries and collect the juice.

Heat the mulled wine in the pot.

Add the agave syrup and cinnamon and simmer for 5 minutes.

Mix cornflour in 4 tbsp juice and add to the simmering mulled wine.

Add the morello cherries.

Layer the gingerbread mousse with the mulled wine cherries in glasses.

PANA COTTA

Ingredients (4 servings)

400 ml soy cream

50 g agave syrup

1 tsp agar agar

1 sachet of vanilla sugar

200 g raspberries (frozen or fresh)

Preparation

Mix all the ingredients, except the raspberries, and bring to a boil slowly in the saucepan.

Simmer for at least one minute for the agar binding.

Pour the liquid into glasses and place in the refrigerator for at least 3 hours.

Puree the raspberries, add a little sugar if desired, and pour over the firm pana cotta.

Of course, strawberries can also be used.

GRILLED CHOCOLATE BANANA

Ingredients

4 bananas

100 g vegan chocolate

2 tbsp. lemon juice

Some (rapeseed) oil

Preparation

Preheat the grill and brush the grate with oil.

Cut the skin of the bananas and the flesh lengthwise on the top.

Squeeze the lemon juice over the flesh.

Break the chocolate and fill it in the bananas.

Place the bananas with the skin side on the grill and grill until the chocolate melts.

HOT APRICOTS

Ingredients

3 large apricots, halved and pitted

A little grated nutmeg

2 tbsp agave syrup

Preparation

Preheat the oven to 200 degrees convection.

Place the apricot halves with the cut sides in a baking dish.

Pour agave syrup and nutmeg over the apricots and bake in the oven for about 15 minutes.

GRILLED BANANA DESSERT

Ingredients for 2 desserts

2 bananas

2 scoops of vegan vanilla ice cream

Chopped peanuts in caramel (vegan)

Preparation

Preheat the grill.

Grill the bananas, in their skins, over medium heat for about 10 minutes, turning frequently.

Slice the bananas lengthwise on a plate and flatten with a fork.

Add the vanilla ice cream and serve garnished with the chopped peanuts in caramel.

CREPES

Ingredients for 6 crepes

100 g flour

200 ml soy drink

1 shot of sparkling mineral water

Nutmeg

1 pinch of salt

(Rapeseed) oil for frying

Preparation

Mix all the ingredients, except the oil, into a smooth batter and leave to soak for 10 minutes.

Brush a pan with oil and heat.

Pour a portion of batter into the pan and spread it around the pan.

Fry the dough on both sides until light brown.

STRAWBERRY SORBET

Ingredients (4 servings)

600 g strawberries, frozen

70 g sugar

300 ml water

2 lemons

Preparation

Squeeze the lemons into a bowl.

Bring the water, sugar, and 6 tbsp lemon juice to a boil in a saucepan.

Stir until the sugar has dissolved.

Leave the lemon syrup to cool.

Finely purée the strawberries with the syrup.

Season to taste with the remaining lemon juice.

Place in the freezer for 15 minutes.

Shape the strawberry sorbet with an ice cream scoop and serve.

COCONUT CHIA PUDDING

Ingredients (2 servings)

200 ml coconut drink

8 tbsp chia seeds

½ tsp vanilla sugar

2 tablespoons sugar

2 tbsp chopped vegan dark chocolate

Preparation

Mix the coconut drink with vanilla sugar.

Stir in chia seeds

Add all the remaining ingredients, mix well and chill.

Leave to soak for 40 minutes. Stir occasionally.

Serve well chilled.

BAKED BANANA

Ingredients (2 servings)

2 bananas

2 tbsp chia seeds

1 tbsp agave syrup

1 tbsp breadcrumbs

1 pinch cinnamon

1 pinch of vanilla sugar

(Coconut) oil for frying

Preparation

Cut the peeled bananas in half lengthwise.

Spread the bananas with agave syrup.

Combine remaining ingredients, except oil.

Roll the bananas in the mixture.

Heat the oil in a pan and fry the bananas in it.

Serve the baked bananas garnished with chia seeds.

COCONUT MILK RICE WITH RASPBERRIES

Ingredients (4 servings)

For the rice pudding

100 g rice

1 tsp grated lemon zest

2 tablespoons sugar

500 ml low-fat coconut milk

1 tsp cinnamon

1 sachet of vanilla sugar

For garnishing

150 g raspberries

Preparation

Bring all the rice pudding ingredients except the rice to a boil in the saucepan.

Add the rice and cook over low heat, stirring occasionally.

Leave to soak for 40 minutes.

Purée the raspberries and pass them through a kitchen sieve.

Fill the coconut milk rice into glasses and garnish with the raspberry puree.

SWEET COUSCOUS

Ingredients (4 servings)

400 g couscous, prepared according to the package instructions

8 dates (pitted)

1 pomegranate

5 tbsp sultanas

Hot water for swelling the sultanas

4 tbsp flaked almonds

3 tablespoons butter

3 tbsp. orange juice

4 tsp cinnamon

2 tbsp agave syrup

1 pinch of salt

4 tbsp icing sugar for garnish

Preparation

Put the sultanas in a bowl and pour hot water over them and leave to soak.

Remove the red fruit seeds from the pomegranate and cut the dates into eighths.

Toast the flaked almonds in a pan without fat until light brown.

Stir the butter into the finished couscous.

Drain the sultanas and leave them to drain.

Mix all the ingredients, except the icing sugar, with the couscous.

Portion onto small, warmed bowls and serve dusted with icing sugar.

Salads

RED CABBAGE SALAD "IN A JIFFY

Ingredients (4 servings)

½ head red cabbage

300 g carrots

1 Apple

4 tbsp lime juice

6 tbsp orange juice

4 tbsp (rapeseed) oil

1 tsp salt

½ teaspoon curry powder

Preparation

Clean the carrots and apples, and core the apples.

Clean the red cabbage and cut it into large pieces.

Put all the ingredients in the blender.

Chop coarsely for 4 seconds on low and push down with a spoon.

Chop again for 4 seconds on medium speed.

WHITE CABBAGE SALAD

Ingredients (4 servings)

½ white cabbage

3 carrots

1 tbsp white wine vinegar

1 tbsp (rapeseed) oil

½ tsp salt

½ tsp pepper

Chives to garnish

Preparation

Cut the white cabbage into fine strips, and finely grate the carrots.

Mix all the ingredients.

Garnish with chives and leave to infuse in the fridge for 2 hours.

BEAN SALAD

Ingredients (4 servings)

1 can of white beans

1 Apple

1 Orange

1 onion

2 tsp mustard

1 tsp thyme

1- 2 tbsp white wine vinegar

4 tbsp (rapeseed) oil

½ tsp pepper

½ tsp salt

Preparation

Pour the beans into a sieve, rinse well and drain.

Put the beans in a salad bowl.

Cut the orange and apple into small pieces, and finely dice the onion.

Mix the orange, apple, onion, and thyme with the beans.

In a separate bowl, mix the oil, vinegar, mustard, salt, and pepper and pour over the salad.

Leave the salad to stand in the fridge for an hour.

BEETROOT SALAD

Ingredients (4 servings)

1 package beetroot, cooked and peeled

1 handful walnuts

1 handful of dried plums

1 clove of garlic

1 tsp salt

1 tsp sugar

Preparation

Press the garlic clove and grate the beetroot.

Mix all the ingredients.

Leave to infuse in the fridge for at least 2 hours.

BULGUR SALAD

Ingredients (4 servings)

1 bunch of spring onions

300 g bulgur

300 ml tomato juice

300 ml water

3 tablespoons parsley

4 tbsp peanuts

1 pinch cinnamon

1 pinch of pepper

1 pinch of salt

7 tbsp (rapeseed) oil

Preparation

Cut the spring onion into fine rings.

Heat the oil in a frying pan and sauté the spring onion.

Add the bulgur and sauté for 2 minutes over medium heat.

Add water, tomato juice, salt, and pepper.

Simmer the bulgur for 10 minutes, covered, over low heat.

Roast the peanuts in a pan.

Sprinkle with cinnamon and roast.

Mix the parsley and peanuts into the bulgur and serve hot.

Drinks

JAGERTEE

Ingredients for 1,5 l

500 ml black tea, prepared according to package instructions
500 ml vegan red wine
150 ml vegan brown rum
250 ml orange juice
Juice of one lemon
1 orange, sliced
6 cloves
1 cinnamon stick

Preparation

Pour the black tea, red wine, orange juice, cinnamon, and cloves into a saucepan and heat, but do not boil!

When the mixture is hot, add the rum, lemon juice, and orange slices.

Heat again until just before boiling. Turn off the heat and leave the Jagertee to infuse for a few hours.

Reheat before serving.

DELICIOUS ORANGE PUNCH

Ingredients for 1 l punch

1000 ml orange juice

2 cinnamon sticks

1 clove

1-star anise

200 ml vegan cream

1 sachet of vanilla sugar

1 sachet vegan cream stiffener

1 untreated orange

Preparation

First, put the orange juice into a pot. Season the orange juice with cinnamon, cloves, and star anise. Heat the whole thing gently.

In the meantime, prepare the cream. Whip the cream with the vanilla sugar, the cream stiffener, and the orange zest until stiff.

Then fill the punch into glasses and cover with the creamy whipped cream. The punch is best served nice and warm.

A PFEL - AMARETTO PUNCH

Ingredients

1000 ml apple juice
1 apple, cored and cut into small cubes
Peel an orange
1 cinnamon stick
8 tbsp vegan amaretto

Preparation

Warm all the ingredients, except the amaretto, gently in the saucepan for 15 minutes.

Pour into cups and add one to two tablespoons of amaretto to taste.

EXOTIC MULLED WINE

Ingredients for 6 cups

1-liter vegan red wine

2 sticks cinnamon

3 cloves

1 orange, sliced

Juice of one lemon

3 tbsp agave syrup

1 tablespoon sugar

Some fresh ginger

A dash of vegan white rum

Preparation

Heat all the ingredients in the pot, but do not let them boil.

Mulled wine is best served nice and warm.

CHILDREN'S PUNCH

Ingredients for 6 punch glasses

500 ml water

500 ml apple juice

1-liter elderberry juice

4 oranges, sliced

Grated lemon zest of one lemon

1 cinnamon stick

4 cloves

Preparation

Bring the water to a boil in the pot.

Add the lemon zest, cinnamon, and cloves, and turn off the heat.

In the second pot, slowly heat the apple and elderberry juices. The juices must not boil! Add the orange slices and turn off the heat.

After about 10 minutes, carefully pour the pots together and leave to infuse for a few hours.

Reheat before serving.

MULLED WINE

Ingredients for 6 cups

1000 ml vegan red wine

1 orange, sliced

2 sticks cinnamon

3 cloves,

Sugar to taste

Preparation

Heat all the ingredients in the pot, but do not let them boil.

Mulled wine is best served nice and warm.

VANILLA WINTER DRINK

Ingredients for 2 cups

100 g cashew nuts (soaked overnight)
350 ml almond drink
4 tbsp agave syrup
1 tsp cinnamon
1/2 tsp nutmeg
1 tsp vanilla sugar

Preparation

Blend all the ingredients and bring to a boil in a saucepan.

Stir occasionally and simmer gently for a few minutes.

Pour into cups while still warm and enjoy.

PUNCH WITH COFFEE

Ingredients for 4 cups

800 ml of hot coffee

2 teaspoons grated orange zest

2 pinch cinnamon

2 pinch clove powder

2 pack vanilla sugar

12 cl vegan liqueur (to taste)

4 Orange slices for garnish

Preparation

Mix all the ingredients, except the liqueur, and leave to infuse briefly.

Pour punch into cups and add liqueur (to taste).

Garnish the punch with orange slices and serve immediately.

WHITE MULLED WINE

Ingredients for 6 cups

1.5-liter vegan white wine

1 Orange

150 ml orange juice

80 ml vegan rum

4 cloves

4 tablespoons sugar

Preparation

Slowly heat all the ingredients in the pot, but do not let them boil.

Remove the cloves before serving.

The white mulled wine is best served nice and warm.

GROG

Ingredients for 1 jar

150 ml water
5 cl vegan rum
2 tsp agave syrup
1 squeeze of lemon juice

Preparation

Pour boiling water into a cup.

Add the rum, agave syrup, and lemon juice.

Grog is best served nice and warm.

GOLDEN MILK

Ingredients for 2 glasses

250 ml vegetable drink to taste

1 tbsp turmeric

1 tsp coconut oil

2 pinches ginger

½ tsp cinnamon

1 pinch nutmeg

1 pinch of pepper

Agave syrup if desired (sweeten to your taste)

Preparation

Mix all the ingredients.

Heat together in a saucepan, but do not boil.

KIWI BANANA SMOOTHIE

Ingredients for 2 glasses

1 ripe banana

2 ripe kiwis

250 ml coconut drink

1 tbsp lemon juice (preferably freshly squeezed)

Preparation

Mix all ingredients for about one minute.

Imprint

© Valerja Rocha

2022

ISBN: 9798840507926

1st edition

Contact: Markus Mägerle/ Am Kreisgraben 17/ 93104 Riekofen/ Germany

Printed in Great Britain
by Amazon

33671217R00073